When the Walls Cave In

poems by

Victoria Dym

Finishing Line Press
Georgetown, Kentucky

When the Walls Cave In

Copyright © 2018 by Victoria Dym
ISBN 978-1-63534-380-9 First Edition
All rights reserved under International and Pan-American Copyright Conventions.
No part of this book may be reproduced in any manner whatsoever without written permission from the publisher, except in the case of brief quotations embodied in critical articles and reviews.

ACKNOWLEDGMENTS

"Yesterday," *Voices from the Attic*, Vol. XVII, edited by Jan Beatty, Carlow University Press, 2011
"POX," *Voices from the Attic*, Vol. XIX, edited by Jan Beatty, Carlow University Press, 2013
"The Bath" and "Eating Shlosta with Granma Bungie," Adanna's Women and Food issue, *Adanna Literary Journal*, Editors, Diane Lockward, Lynne McEniry, Christine Redman-Waldeyer, April 2014
"Blood Clot," "No Air for Any of It," and "You Know How September Can Be," published online by Euonia Review, permanent link, https://eunoiareview.wordpress.com/2013
"When the Walls Cave In, First Place Poetry Prize, *10 Carlow University's MFA Anniversary Anthology*, Carlow University Press, 2014
"Thin," *Voices from the Attic*, Vol. XVI, edited by Jan Beatty, Carlow University Press, 2010
"Shift," *Voices from the Attic,* Vol. XX, edited by Jan Beatty, Carlow University Press, 2014
"Bird Song," published online by Terri Wolverton, *Writers at Work*, permanent link, https://writersatwork.wordpress.com/2012
"Your Lips, My Lips," published in *Voices from the Attic*, Vol. XV, edited by Jan Beatty, Carlow University Press, 2009
"You May Not Know," published in *Dionne's Story*, Vol. 1, an anthology of poetry and prose for the awareness of violence against women, edited by Angela Bayout, Carlow University Press, 2009
"The Fight" published for *Broadsides Poetry Off the Shelf* 2016, broadside publication, art gallery showing, and reading, January 2016, Fort Myers, Florida

Publisher: Leah Maines
Editor: Christen Kincaid
Cover Art: Pat Collins
Author Photo: Calvin Knight/ LKLDtv.com
Cover Design: Elizabeth Maines McCleavy

Printed in the USA on acid-free paper.
Order online: www.finishinglinepress.com
also available on amazon.com

Author inquiries and mail orders:
Finishing Line Press
P. O. Box 1626
Georgetown, Kentucky 40324
U. S. A.

Table of Contents

Yesterday 1
Eating Shlosta with Granma Bungie 2
The FC Land 3
Pox 4
Paper Pudding 5
No Air for Any of It 6
The Bath 7
When the Walls Cave In 8
On the N9 9
Trinity Pets 10
Found 11
Wart 12
Lessons from the Laundry Room 13
You Know How September Can Be 14
We Used To Walk These Woods Together 15
The Fight 16
Thin 17
Soup 18
Impingement Haiku 19
Blood Clot 20
Defenestration 21
Clean Sweep Sonnet 23
Shift 24
Bird Song 25
You May Not Know 26
Celeste Brings Me Seashells 27
Your Lips, My Lips 28
Unrequited 29
Summer Crossing 30
For Rent on Anawanda 31
Wish 32
The End of the World 33

for Marygrace…..
         who knows

Yesterday
    for Hilda Doolittle

the rain came down
in drowning pools,
jellyfish reaching
their jellyfish tendrils
toward the earth
like lightning streamers,
flashy screamers
across the lungfish clouds,
floating low
breathing dark all day
in the sad sea-sky of gray.
like the inside of my womb,
murky, watery depths
godlike winds,
immortal salt
from where the tears burst
forth like microburst
from lack of light,
the umbrella upended,
inside out like
a jellyfish,
like my womb
rooting for
plankton.

Eating Shlosta with Granma Bungie

Swirled glass Pepsi bottles on the padded white tablecloth;
she pours into the opalescent pitcher. She stirs the gasses
from the syrup, slips the flat liquid into shot glasses.
My brother and I drink: *L' chaim!*
The huge mahogany circa 1930's dining set, the sideboard
and glass hutch with its gleaming crystal contents,
she takes her coffee, heavy with sugar and cream.
Sometimes we have her *Hamantaschen* cookies:
three corners oozing with apricot, cherry, prune
or poppy seed, sometimes fresh baked bread
with strawberry jam, fruit from the truck that
delivers on Flemington Street on Fridays.
Sometimes Granma Bungie makes stinky cheese.
Shlosta, she says in Russian-Polish. Farmer's
cheese that hangs in slings and drips to the sink,
cloth fastened to the handle of the cabinet above.
It takes days for the whey to drip away.
What's left: dried curd, and when unwrapped,
the white cheese is covered with a green hair-like mold.
Granma Bungie mixes in butter, eggs, and salt—scrambles.

The FC Land

I'm singing the song of my childhood living room,
where the nickname *FC Land* is coined by a friend named *Chu*.

I'm singing the name of the dog who raised me: the lure of collie
dander, musty fur and warm belly. She sleeps on a braided rug

by the front door like a draft catcher, her name, Eustacia;
I curl up like her pup.

I'm singing the song of the camel saddle, a show piece
that gathers weekly dust with the other knickknacks

on the grey stone mantel. I ride in secret to wild exotic
desert locations; the brass posts transform, two dromedary humps.

I'm singing the praises for the Ed Sullivan show,
Topo Gigio and Jerry Lewis, for my father's painting

of Eustacia as a whiteface clown, for my mother's
Manhattans, strong with two cherries.

I'm singing the song of the Italian frosted glass coffee table
with the brass legs that I clean on Saturday, Brasso polish,

like a perfume that stays under my nail beds well into the next week.
The songs of chores, swing low, swing high.

I'm singing the song of the family-sized bag of Snyder's potato chips.
My brother eats the entire 64 ounces by himself with a 2-liter of Coke.

Later he feigns his suicide: ketchup on his tee shirt, knife at his side,
he lies in wait for me to find.

POX

running away from the gorilla:
apish breath so close and moist, and me, running,
running, my small feet tripping over rotating terrains: trees,
hallways, animated throbbing backdrops—
the breath— fear, like the grape that sticks in the throat.

And then, the witch's hand, all gnarled, bony
wrinkled green, with long cracked and dirty nails
grabs for tiny ankles from underneath the bed—

Mother ties my hands and feet to the bed

so I won't scratch the chicken pox— won't leave a
mark on my face.

Paper Pudding

Ink that smells like lovemaking, stationery in the desk drawer,
pastel blue, rose, yellow, the reams of typewriter white

It's all like pudding—paper pudding
the forest, saplings and mature trees, cut and shipped to the city, the paper mill.

It's the full cycle. It's Magee Women's Hospital in Pittsburgh, one month
early, Eat N Park and large breasts, Eleanor and Leo, Dyms and Davis'

alcoholics, and graduates, *Go to your room*, and *Shut up*, Catholics and
Jews, Unitarian Universalists, and cocktails at brunch. *Do unto others,*

as they would do unto you, Stinky Cheese and pierogies, paper and ash,
cigarettes that killed both parents, the deer that cracked my father's ribs

the car with the constant smoke stream, my mother who would never turn the
other cheek, diaphragm that failed, kept in the nightstand all those years, cracked

and dry. That childhood piano, Twinkle Twinkle; it's the day I chop it,
cracked and dry—wood pieces that turn to paper.

No Air for Any of It

Her gown comes undone from the back, her shoulder bare,
drooping breasts at 64, unwashed since Tuesday, her hair.

She seems happy in the hospital, propped up, chatty.
She talks about hospital life, her dogs and cigarettes.

She gets shaky then, like she does when she need a drink
(I'd been making them for her, Manhattans, straight up,

just as she'd ordered, since I was 12). Morphine drip, and this smell:
a mix of industrial cleaner, body odor and urine; she has peed

the bed. I watch as her hazel eyes bug out, her lips open and still.
She is trying to speak or scream— there is no air for any of it.

She is paralyzed in massive coronary, and for the
first time, to me, vulnerable, oddly beautiful, my Mother.

The Bath

There was a time
when you waited like the cats,
for me to appear from the bath:

> mandarin orange or lavender sweet
> thighs and buttocks, breasts and back
> delicious hot cup of bergamot black,

from primordial soup
like a tadpole, like Venus,
perfumed and nude.

When the Walls Cave In

You can't see or hear
the geese overhead, flying in formation
the most perfect honking 'V'

When the walls cave in,
snowfall means heartache, not
the jazz dance of frozen love

There is only minutia,
cracks and holes and empty want—
hiccups, rashes, ingrown hairs

I am living my life in Paris
even though I have not yet arrived there.
After a luxurious salted morning bath,
I take the Metro 10
decide on *pain au raisin* and *croissants*,
shop the outdoor markets for berries
relax with a cup of Lilly of the Valley tea
at Café Flore, before a rose petal facial

When the walls cave in,
you can only stand where you are
choke on tears, forget to bathe

You can't climb the Eiffel Tower,
or visit the Louvre; you can't smell
the lavender from the fields of Provence

There is only grey rubble
and a beating of drums that pound
a sorrowful dirge which wraps

like twine around your ankles

On the N9

It happens: white and grey farm cat, thrashes about the middle solid line,
hit by a driver from the opposite traffic that rushes like the very blood in
beast and man. I am in a tour bus to Bloomsday, equidistant

from the hit, the cat still thrashes, the cars still rush. Does the offender
even know of the offense, of the rush in my heart, as we both
travel the road further in time and space? Perhaps the other driver denies

it was him or doesn't know. If he felt the breaking feline bones against
his right fender, does he think, *there is nothing I can do?* The cars still
rush. Does he think, *it happens: just a white and grey farm cat on the N9.*

Trinity Pets

Halfway between work and home, twice each day, the subway stops in front of Trinity Pets. Live and frozen mice are for sale; Gators held till Xmas, Chihuahua puppies, and a 'Buy one, get one free' on rabbits. The signs in the window change with the inventory, and I think about the goings-on in the small store; the phone rings intermittently because the number posted out front, *531-PETS* is so compelling. I imagine the Chihuahuas and the gators in cages, looking at each other from across the room, from different parts of the globe, waiting for, hoping for and dreaming of Chihuahua love or gator love. I think about the live mice; if they are sold next to their frozen counterparts. Some nights, coming home later on the subway, the cages are backlit, outlines behind the sign in the window: *Valentine's Day Special, 2 lovebirds with cage, $150.*

Found

(Mama cat lived under our Saturn
in the driveway most nights,
same black stripes and white markings,
swaying pregnant teats,
just seen begging at the tavern
beside the post office Wednesday)

The fur does not jump
no kitten crazies
no cries like a baby
this fur is silent   still
        dead kitten.

Back legs splayed
muzzle to the ground
black fly round the eye
now milk-white
ants crawl along the spine
measuring both width and length.

Wart

It's at the crown of his head,
my black cat, I worry about it—
Just a wart, says the vet. *Don't worry.*
But I do. Imagine the growth getting potato-sized
with roots grabbing downward into brain matter,
like fingers, spreading, playing in Jell-O.

I worry about falling—out of bed,
down the stairs, on the street,
falling in a foreign country.
All of these have already happened,
so I worry even more.

I worry that I'll never find another love;
have *sweet sex* in the morning,
feel the pangs the next day; worry that
I become homeless, live under a bridge,
worry that I'll never see Paris,

or if I do—I fall on the Champs des Élysées,
near the Arc de Triomphe, break a hip.
I worry the mirror about my ugly American body,
about not telling the truth. I worry about randomness
and extreme order. Wonder and worry about vegans—
worry too about becoming a crazy cat lady.

My tan cat has a growth as well.
At the base of his spine, a bit
to the right—right before his tail starts.
I worry that this is not a wart—
Is it growing—getting bigger?

Lessons from the Laundry Room

The prospect of clean sheets—
putting a load in before work,
Mook slips into the litterbox.

The Christmas card, pants pocket,
from Rosemary in Sun City West,
(she played my mother once)

white hair now, she stands, retired
beside an 8' inflatable snowman
in the desert, smiling—

or is that just the fold of the paper?
Cat scratches the basement floor.
Photo letter goes to recycling.

The rescued Maine Coon looks at me,
I at him. He always poops whenever I do
laundry, and chortles, slightly high-pitched

as the washing machine rumbles,
like a prophet.   Years later, I find
a cell phone in Larry's gym bag with only

one name in the contacts. I am in the
laundry room with his soiled underwear
while he is out fucking someone from church.

You Know How September Can Be

You know how September can be—
a wide-eyed insect, well-veined jar fly,
spittlebug, locust. Eaten chocolate covered
or in a pie with cream and rhubarb,
stir-fried, breaded. It's the cicada— his song
so loud it makes the Chinese Emperor in me swoon.
In the wee hours, I am my former self: exoskeleton,
DNA left in trees, immortalized on a brick wall,
stuck to the sidewalk.

We Used To Walk These Woods Together

in the hollow near the creek, deer path—

imagine here, the hammer-bludgeoned body, the Halloween night nightmare
the low scratchy beat of headphones too loud—bed bugs & their eggs living in
the recovered mattress stashed in the brush.

*Meet me here in the
clearing—I want my tee shirt back.*

We used to walk these woods together hand in hand, following the path,
shade cool forest, the occasional hollow caw caw of a crow,
squirrels squirreling to and fro.

*Let's take a walk to the store—
put some in the money tree.*

We used to walk these woods, a hole-hollow in the big oak,
we started the myth, sprites at night, many found a penny, some silver coins,
magic mana deep in the hollow near the creek, deer path—

We used to walk these woods, never imagining the arrest warrant posted, hot
orange, you haven't passed this way in years—high school lovers met here too.
Love is not so easy to end, especially if one is not ready go.

*What's happening with
kids these days—so hollow on the inside.*

What has become of you and I, now public record.
We used to walk, deer path—

The Fight

The weather inside these words we speak:
the breathing tornado that
swirls sixty miles per hour winds
collects siding and roofs
car parts and body parts
garden dirt and photo albums

This morning was ashes and there wasn't any rain.

How many years have we been doing this together?
the same vaudeville, the cheeky burlesque
this show that not only entertains but sustains
a nourishing scam, the perfect last meal

We have decided now to free the doves.

Thin

Rotten, and now, light comes in at night straight through
because everything is so goddamn thin—my eyelids,
toenails, blood—the light from the street lamp through the sheers
burning two shafts on the ceiling, through me, thin like towers.

Thin like twins, lying side by side in baby thin sleep,
like paper thin sleep—the veil between what is,
what could be, and what has been—so thin—
light comes in.

Soup

I eat soup with my hands now, right from the pot; never mind the heat.
An occasional pea, noodle or carrot is caught;
the broth pours away through fingers that once held

your face, caressed your cheek, full of tears; and soup trickles—
the preamble for cats: *Get down from the dinner table,*
pointing fingers wave down, my chin to the floor,

down through the foundation, a spongy, sphagnum moss of eggshells
and nettles. Now, I walk the marital house like a widow, no
surefootedness, holes in the carpet, my shirt, your excuses;

holes and pinpoints of chaos, shafts of dusty ache, like jagged soup can
punches to the gut. Here, I walk to the mailbox; the mortgage is due.
Then I walk to the cupboard to inventory the cans. Someday,

invisible to me now as my own heartbeat—a stew from scratch:
fresh herbs, chicken, potatoes—a spoon.

Impingement Haiku

    Giant octopus
tree roots—cat's claws dig deep down:
    pain nests in shoulder.

Blood Clot

She holds my hand in the pulse pose,
forces me to read poetry to her.

She checks my breathing, stethoscope
cold on my back like the barrel of a pistol—

she confesses that if she had not become
a physician, she would have been a poet.

Defenestration
after the works of John Baldessari

Colors burst forth,
    red   orange   yellow
cardboard rectangles, physically thrown out, attic window
    green   blue   violet.

The banal, the artistic, photographed, framed, aligned:
white clapboard house of Baldessari himself
    photographed by him.

What would you throw out your window?
    words   letters from lovers
themselves flown.

What are the rules of art, of marriage, of life?
puff of smoke imitates a cloud:
    a cloud resembles the brain.

Hands pointing, words pointing, look:
    here   now.
Stand on one foot,
the tension like a knife to the neck,
    to the elbow, to the one foot not touching the ground.

There isn't anytime

Throw something out the window *now*.

Smell the fresh cut grass, the warm brownie,
the black bean soup— paint the room: lizard green,
with frog's belly, spinach, then American cheese or
    a perky peach for the trim.

Select any adjective to describe your facial expression.

My personal faves: Popeyed—Pure Beauty.

            and

Don't forget the paperclips.
Let everything of virtue and vice
pile up on the sidewalk.
        Xmas for garbage men.

Clean Sweep Sonnet

my ex comes to the house—
keeps his key a secret   (when no one is there)

he plans it so he can clown
with Mook, our Maine Coon—vacuums—

yet another thing he misses—
repeats this behavior every chance he gets

every chance since he left—
every chance since he was found out

until *this* time— instead of putting it away—
He leaves the vacuum out.

I think, at first, coming through the basement
there's a burglar in the house, and then I'm sure

it is not a vacuum robber, but simply a man
who is in the habit of sneaking around.

Shift

    Hoarse crocuses, violets with respiratory ailments,
today high sixties,
        the smell of air-dried
    linens, a subtle calm, under currents of revolution but,
clean sailing through to Fall's maize. How amazing
      to fall back, spring ahead.
    Sixty minutes of daylight savings time,
forwards or back when nothing
        and nobody in the world dies,
                not even a worm.

Bird Song
for Sydney

Waiting out winter like
waiting for a phone call,
half past February…

like a ring tone
in the name of Spring,
we hear this warbling.

That one, you say,
that's my fave…
and instantly, I hear

the bird song, as I see
you, sitting on the couch,
eyes closed, listening,

teacup in hand, smiling…
a thin break in the eggshell:
beak behind your lips.

You May Not Know

my love, what love I had for you:
like the ant buried in the peony,

You may not know that it would have gotten better.
That just like farmers till their fields

we could have worked on it—
that there were two blue speckled

robin's eggs in the nest that morning,
that we could have cozied up to each other

played ping pong through the night
laughed and added years to our lives, instead.

You may not know that honesty is everything
that how to tell the truth is how to love

that even flaws are charmers, if you are true.
What you may not know

is that I will love again,
I will catch myself in a shop window and think

how sexy, how hot my naturally fetching smile
and even if no other man will ever have me,

I will please myself and speak to myself
in long loving whispers and with poetry; and all will know

that the finishing touches were my hands
on our daughter, teaching her to lie with

only those that can regale beauty,
like the sunflower forever following the sun.

Celeste Brings Me Seashells

Shells rest like hands in hands.
Nest like Matryoshka dolls,
one inside the next—
scallop fans from the deep blue.

And when the birds fall,
sacs of fluid and cartilage
covered in feathers
drop thump to the ground.

And when the squirrels fall,
sacs of fluid and cartilage
covered in fur
drop thump also to the ground,

except with more heft, more breadth.
Like Henny Penny, in concentric circles
I run—phone Celeste—stack the shells,
as she asks softly, Is your sky falling?

And I tell her, bird by bird,
squirrel by squirrel—
soon we are talking about
tennis, the rain, Paul Durcan,

in-home vacuuming systems, the deep dark—
She passes The Dogbone House,
still talking—the dog park—still barking,
to the beach where she finds the shells.

Your Lips, My Lips

Aperture of love,
your lips swell—
speaking, puckering
two pillows, bedded
capillaries of arousal,
flash of creamy white
flute sounds,
wet and moist
as berries.

I want to come
to know the world
through my lips only—
to kiss my way through
landscapes, countries,
literature and men,
to kiss your lips now—
pressing and resting
pressing and resting.

Unrequited

I plant my heart
still beating
deep in the soil of your chest

No pain:
your eyes lock mine—
anesthesia

Poetry sutures, I kiss —
my lips, stitch your incision
close it, with no scar

My chest remains open
a gaping, hollow wound
that you refuse to love

Summer Crossing

cool sweater morning

children with backpacks

waiting at August's cliffside

—at the precipice of school—

the last strands of lazy days

like the spider we watched dangling

between the red maple and the porch

a female, pouched belly and spikes

—each day a nature show

before you left—

now boats cut the water

barge, motor, canoe

colors of white and sunlight

the web of the everyday river

below

I cross above twice daily on the train

For Rent on Anawanda Street

I am looking

for a place to live—

a way of life

with a door that locks

and room for small pets

and books

and love

a dishwasher

and beauty—

a garage

an address

of happiness

and windows—

(preferably with a view).

Wish

Court me with sweet almond
calla lilies and jasmine

Speak to me in love's
whispers—call me *beauty*

Rekindle the sultry
Rekindle the kindness

Show me fireworks and
sunsets in your eyes

Make your half-truths whole
slowly and softly unwrap

Take my hand in patience
Let us be together again

Come to me anew

The End of the World

The iPhone makes a low and scratchy sound, and then a high pitched whine
—the touchpad goes fuzzy like the old black and white televisions.
A ringtone of sorts—I press the home button to prove I am not dreaming
—my mother, dead now twenty two years, fades in and out of vision.

*I hope that you are with someone you like and that you are doing
something important because the end of the world is tomorrow.*
The phone goes hot, then cold in my hand—4:24 AM, Saturday.

The cat curls perfectly at my feet—a deep sigh. I rub his back with my right
foot, careful not to disturb him. He stretches, then curls his white-booted
paw, buries his head further into the coverlet. In a bit, I will dress, go out to
the garden, watch the sunrise, and snatch a lima bean pod & a cherry tomato.

I will brush my hand against the lavender leaves, crush jasmine flowers
between my fingers and inhale. For some reason, I am craving tacos and
beans and rice. Later for dinner, I plan to walk to the restaurant which is

over two miles away. (I've driven enough in my life.) Should I call my daughter
to relay my mother's message? I decide to text instead: *I love you* ~Mom, with
a heart emoji replacing the 'o' in Mom—(That has been my signature for texting
with my daughter since the beginning of texting). No need to alarm her—she

lives her life like me—I am confident that she **is** with someone she likes and no
doubt, she **is** doing something important. I try not to stress her out in general.
My best friend, Barbara, will call, or I will call her. We talk at least once a day.

She's retired now in Pittsburgh. I'll read her this poem and she will say—*Cool*,
as she always does. I will tell her that I love her, as I always do—she won't say
it back, but I know that she does. After dinner— I'll watch the sunset and the
moon rise, try to find Orion's belt, the North Star, hope for the Big Dipper—

I think about contacting you, my love, but decide against it—
we've already said our goodbyes months ago.

Victoria Dym is a graduate of Ringling Brother's Barnum and Bailey Clown College with a degree in Humility. She has also earned a Bachelor of Arts, in Philosophy, from the University of Pittsburgh, and her Masters in Fine Arts in Creative Writing-Poetry at Carlow University. Her poetry has been published in various anthologies, including *Voices in the Attic, Dionne's Story, Pearl Magazine, Girls with Glasses,* and *Adanna Literary Journal,* as well as in the *Pittsburgh Post-Gazette,* and the *City Paper.* Find Victoria's poems online at the *Writer's at Work* site, *Eunoia Review, Rat's Ass Review, Terrene,* and *flash glass* 2017.

Victoria won first prize and publication for her poem, "When The Walls Cave In" in *10, Carlow University's MFA Anniversary Anthology.* Ms Dym's poem "The Fight" was selected for *Broadsides Poetry off the Shelf 2016,* broadside publication, art gallery showing, and reading, January 2016 in Fort Myers, Florida. Her chapbook, *Class Clown,* was chosen as one of ten finalists in the Coal Hill Review Chapbook Contest, by Autumn Hill Press, and ultimately published by Finishing Line Press in 2015. Ms. Dym has taught poetry as a Guest Lecturer at Seton Hill University, at Winterim, through the Western Pennsylvania Writing Program in conjunction with the University of Pittsburgh, at Mellon Middle School as a Poet in Person, at Keep St. Pete Lit, and Polk State University. Victoria co-organized Writer's in the Woods, a workshop retreat extolling camping, poetry and laughter.

Ms. Dym has an IMDb credit as an actress in three movies, *Dominick and Eugene, Bloodsucking Pharaohs in Pittsburgh,* and *The Man with Elephant Hands.* She also has an IMDb credit as a co-writer for 7 Lives of Chance, 2013, and The Man with Elephant Hands, 2016. Victoria is currently an improviser with the Box Theater, on the team, *Dear Aunt Gertrude* in Tampa Florida. Victoria Dym, a Certified Laughter Yoga Leader, is owner of Laugh Out Loud, a company that specializes in bringing laughter into the workplace, as a regular practice, for corporate meetings, group events, retreats, private parties, and reunions. A good practice for writers, laughter is the best medicine!

www.ingramcontent.com/pod-product-compliance
Lightning Source LLC
LaVergne TN
LVHW041559070426
835507LV00011B/1178